Easy Way Guide
To Signing

*A donation from the sale of this publication, will
be used solely to enhance and advance the
quality of life, of deaf people.*

GW00658066

43 Mansfield Avenue, Thornaby, TS17 7EG
Telephone: (01642) 677844
www.jakbooks.com
email. sales@jakbooks.com

Published by Jak Books Limited
Printed by Remmer Print

A donation from the sale of this publication, will be used solely to enhance and advance the quality of life, of deaf people.

This pocket signing book was created in its entirety, by the young profoundly deaf people named below.

Author
Mr Alan Thompson Jnr

Layout & Graphic Artwork Team
Mr. Alan Thompson
Mr. Arif H. Rehman
Mr Timothy A. V. Teasdale

Originally Created 1993

Re-Created and Published 1997

Re-Published 2002

ISBN 0 9544443 0 2

Name..

Address...

....

....

Special Telephone Numbers

....

....

....

....

....

Notes

....

....

....

....

INTRODUCTION

When hearing people go on holiday in different countries in the world and can't speak the same, hearing people use a book so they can speak the same and can communicate.

The deaf sometime want to talk to hearing people but it is hard for hearing people to understand.

This book was made by deaf people to help the deaf communicate and make it easy in every day things, like when we want a doctor or in a shop, we keep the book in our pocket when it is difficult to sign to someone and they can't understand what we want, we can show them the sign in the book with the word we want to say.

Because the book is small we can use the book to help our family and friends learn to sign anywhere - anytime.

We can also use the book to help us with our word spelling when we want to write letters or leave notes for people.

With this book and people helping and working together, we hope we will understand each other better.

Alan Thompson Jnr Editor
(Born Profoundly Deaf)

CONTENTS

ALPHABET - FINGERSPELLING 1

NUMBER SYSTEM 2-3

COLOUR 4

IMPORTANT SIGNS USED OFTEN 5-8

SIGNS WITH OPPOSITE MEANING 9-18

FAMILY AND PEOPLE 19-22

SIGNS USED IN SCHOOL 23-26

SIGNS FOR MUSIC AND TV 27

TIMES DAYS AND DATES 28-29

SEASONS 30

HOUSE (indoors) 31-34

HOUSE (outside) 35-36

FOOD AND DRINK 37-42

CLOTHES 43-44

ANIMALS 45-48

COUNTRIES AND TOWNS 49-51

BUILDINGS 52

WORK 53

BANK AND SHOPS 54-56

HOSPITAL 57-61

SPORTS 62-63

CHURCH 64-65

LAW 66-67

TRANSPORT AND DRIVING 68-73

ALPHABET A-Z 74-104

DEAF PEOPLE 105

TELEPHONE AND MINICOM FOR THE DEAF 106

INDEX 107-114

A B C D
E F G H
I J K L
M N O P
Q R S T
U V W X
Y Z

0 - ZERO	**1 - ONE**	**2 - TWO**	**3 - THREE**
4 - FOUR	**5 - FIVE**	**6 - SIX**	**7 - SEVEN**
8 - EIGHT	**9 - NINE**	**10 - TEN**	**11 - ELEVEN**
12 - TWELVE	**13 - THIRTEEN**	**14 - FOURTEEN**	**15 - FIFTEEN**
16 - SIXTEEN	**17 - SEVENTEEN**	**18 - EIGHTEEN**	**19 - NINETEEN**

2

NUMBER SYSTEM

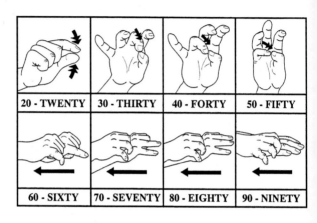

20 - TWENTY	30 - THIRTY	40 - FORTY	50 - FIFTY
60 - SIXTY	70 - SEVENTY	80 - EIGHTY	90 - NINETY

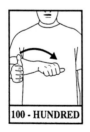

100 - HUNDRED

1,000 - THOUSAND

1,000,000 - MILLION

		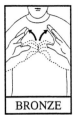	
COLOUR	BLACK	BLUE	BRONZE
	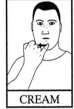	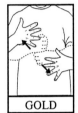	
BROWN	CREAM	GOLD	GREEN
		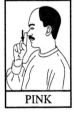	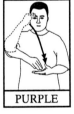
GREY	ORANGE	PINK	PURPLE
		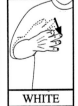	
RED	SILVER	WHITE	YELLOW

4

IMPORTANT SIGNS USED OFTEN

 WHAT

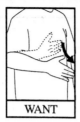 WANT

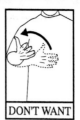 DON'T WANT

 WHICH

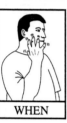 WHEN

 WHERE

 WHO

 HOW

 WHOSE

 WHY

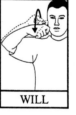 WILL

 WON'T

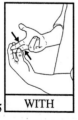 WITH

 WITHOUT

 RIGHT

 WRONG

5

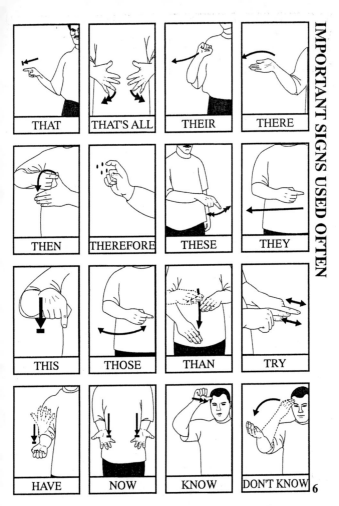

THAT	THAT'S ALL	THEIR	THERE
THEN	THEREFORE	THESE	THEY
THIS	THOSE	THAN	TRY
HAVE	NOW	KNOW	DON'T KNOW

6

I	MY	MINE	MY OWN

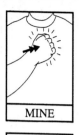 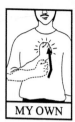  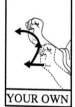

MYSELF	YOU	YOUR	YOUR OWN

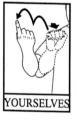 

SELF	YOURSELF	YOURSELVES	HIS

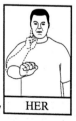 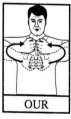 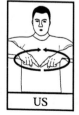 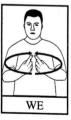

HER	OUR	US	WE

IF	EACH	EVER	EVERY
THING	VERY	MUCH	GET
HERE	MAYBE	MIGHT	PERHAPS
ARE	IS	THEM	WAS

8

SIGNS WITH OPPOSITE MEANING

CAN	CAN'T	AND	BUT
DO	DON'T	DON'T LIKE	LIKE
YES	NO	IN	OUT
BEFORE (past)	BEFORE	AFTER	LATER

9

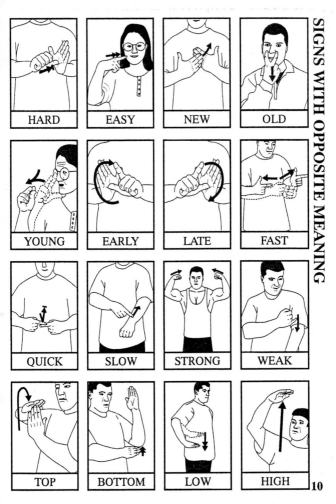

SIGNS WITH OPPOSITE MEANING

HARD | EASY | NEW | OLD

YOUNG | EARLY | LATE | FAST

QUICK | SLOW | STRONG | WEAK

TOP | BOTTOM | LOW | HIGH

10

SIGNS WITH OPPOSITE MEANING

SIT

STAND

INSIDE

OUTSIDE

SEPARATE

TOGETHER

DIFFERENT

SAME

LONG

SHORT

DECREASE

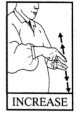
INCREASE

DEEP

SHALLOW

HAPPEN

OCCUR

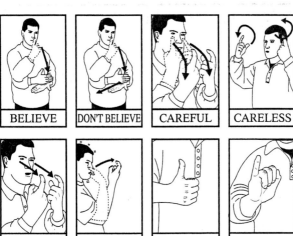
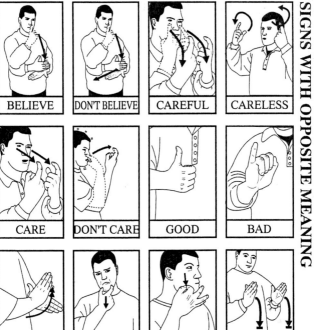

| BELIEVE | DON'T BELIEVE | CAREFUL | CARELESS |

| CARE | DON'T CARE | GOOD | BAD |

| HAPPY | SAD | JUST | MUST |

| PLEASE | THANK YOU | HELLO | BYE ! |

12

SIGNS WITH OPPOSITE MEANING

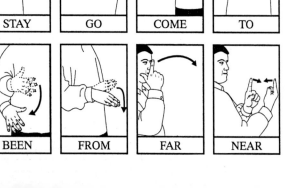

SURE	NOT SURE	GIVE	RECEIVE
BRING	TAKE	ARRIVE	LEAVE
STAY	GO	COME	TO
BEEN	FROM	FAR	NEAR

RUN

WALK

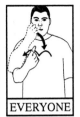
EVERYONE

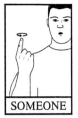
SOMEONE

FORGOT

REMEMBER

FIND

LOSE

HEAVY

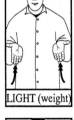
LIGHT (weight)

ROUGH

SMOOTH

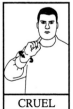
CRUEL

KIND

GENEROUS

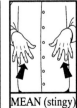
MEAN (stingy)

14

SIGNS WITH OPPOSITE MEANING

ANGRY	PATIENT (clam)	IMPOSSIBLE	POSSIBLE
POLITE	RUDE (manners)	LESS	MORE
SOME	FEW	RICH	POOR
OPEN	SHUT (closed)	EMPTY	FULL

DIRTY	MESS	CLEAN	TIDY

  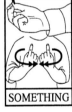 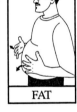

BEST	BETTER	WORSE	WORST

 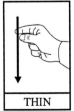  

EVERYTHING	NOTHING	SOMETHING	FAT

THICK	THIN	NARROW	WIDE

16

ABOVE	BELOW	UNDER	OVER
UP	DOWN	AGREE	DISAGREE
ON	OFF	OFTEN	RARELY
START	FINISH	BEGIN	END

BEAUTIFUL	HANDSOME	PRETTY	UGLY
LOVE	HATE	AWFUL	NICE

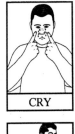   

CRY	JOKE	LAUGH	BIG

 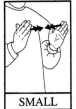  

LITTLE	SMALL	LITTLE (bit)	LOTS

18

FAMILY	GRANDFATHER	GRANDMOTHER	PARENT
FATHER	MOTHER	CHILDREN	DAUGHTER
SON	BROTHER	SISTER	AUNTIE
UNCLE	NEPHEW	NIECE	COUSIN

PEOPLE	ADULT	MR.	MRS.
HUSBAND	WIFE	MAN	WOMAN
CHILD	BOY	GIRL	FRIEND
ARMY	NAVY	SOLDIER	SAILOR

PARTNER

HE

SHE

HIM

HER (indicate)

SINGLE (status)

ENGAGED

MARRY

DIVORCE

BOUNCER

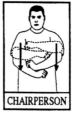

CHAIRPERSON

COMMITTEE

SECRETARY

KING

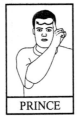

QUEEN

PRINCE

PRINCESS

KNIGHT

SERVANT

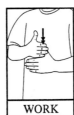

WORK

MANAGER

FOREMAN

WELDER

APPRENTICE

BUTCHER

FARMER

FIREMAN

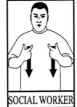

SOCIAL WORKER

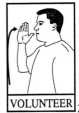

VOLUNTEER

22

 CURRICULUM

 EDUCATION

 SCHOOL

HEADMASTER

 TEACHER

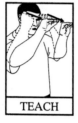 TEACH

 CLASS

 LESSON

 LEARN

 BOOK (a)

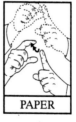 PAPER

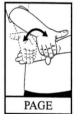 PAGE

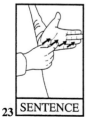 SENTENCE

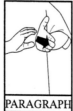 PARAGRAPH

 STORY

 READ

WRITE | ALPHABET | ENGLISH | PEN

PENCIL | RULER | RUBBER | MEASURE

MATHS | ADD | PLUS | MINUS

SUBTRACT | DIVIDE | MULTIPLY | PERCENT

ARITHMETIC

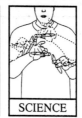

SCIENCE

ART

GRAMMAR

FRACTION

QUARTER

HALF

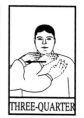

THREE-QUARTER

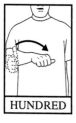

HUNDRED

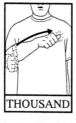

THOUSAND

MILLION

ANGLE

CURVE

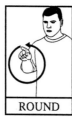

ROUND

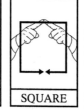

SQUARE

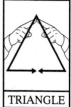

TRIANGLE

ASK	QUESTION	THINK	ANSWER
EXAM	MARK	CLEVER	COLLEGE
LECTURE	UNIVERSITY	QUALIFICATIONS	COMMUNICATE
SIGN	LANGUAGE	FINGER SPELL	INTERPRET

SIGNS FOR MUSIC AND TV

TELEVISION

PROGRAMME

ACT (drama)

FILM

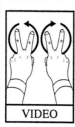

VIDEO

COMPUTER

NOTE (music)

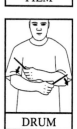

DRUM

GUITAR

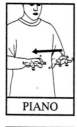

PIANO

XYLOPHONE

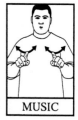

MUSIC

RADIO

SING

DANCE

TRUMPET

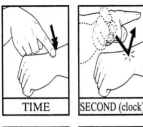
TIME

SECOND (clock)

MINUTE

HOUR

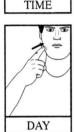
DAY

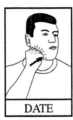
DATE

CALENDAR

EVERY DAY

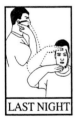
LAST NIGHT

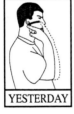
YESTERDAY

TODAY

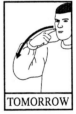
TOMORROW

GOOD MORNING

MORNING

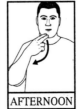
AFTERNOON

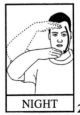
NIGHT

28

WEEKEND

WEEK

FORTNIGHT

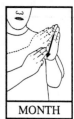

MONTH

LAST WEEK

THIS WEEK

NEXT WEEK

YEAR

LAST YEAR

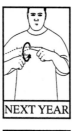

NEXT YEAR

EVENING

SKY

CLOUDS

SUN

MOON

STARS

SEASONS	SPRING	SUMMER	AUTUMN
WINTER	WEATHER	THUNDER	LIGHTNING
WIND	RAIN	SNOW	ICE
FOG	GALE	FROST	

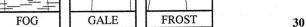

BRICK	HOUSE	ROOF	CHIMNEY
CEILING	BULB	WALL	HALL
STAIRS	ROOM	KITCHEN	DOOR
HANDLE	GLASS	WINDOW	HOME

FURNITURE	CARPET	CURTAIN	BED
BUNK BEDS	DRESSING TABLE	WARDROBE	BLANKET
PILLOW	SHEET	ARMCHAIR	SOFA
FIREPLACE	SIDEBOARD	CHAIR	TABLE

32

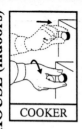
COOKER

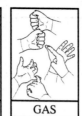
GAS

ELECTRIC

FRIDGE

SINK (kitchen)

WASHING MACHINE

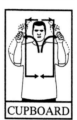
CUPBOARD

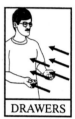
DRAWERS

TRAY

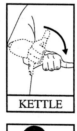
KETTLE

TEAPOT

TEA-SET

PLATE

CUP

SAUCER

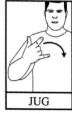
JUG

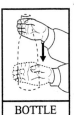

BOWL	DISH	KNIFE	FORK
SPOON	TEASPOON	GLASS (drink)	BOTTLE
JAR	LID	IRON	COOK
BAKE	FRY	GRILL (cook)	MASH

34

GARDEN	GATE	FENCE	HEDGE
GRASS	SEEDS	FLOWER	LEAF
PLANT	GROW	ROOT	BUSH
TREE	BRANCH	SPADE	FIELD

BABY-SIT	HIGHCHAIR
PRAM	PLAY

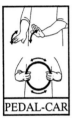 PEDAL-CAR

 SCOOTER (toy)

 JIGSAW

 SKIPPING ROPE

 PARK

 KITE

 SLIDE

 FOREST

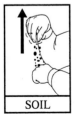 SOIL

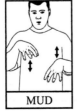 MUD

 POND

 STONE

36

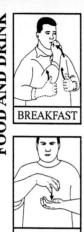 BREAKFAST

 CORNFLAKES

 MEAL

 BREAD

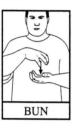 BUN

 BUTTER

 HOT DOG

 CHEESE

 EGG

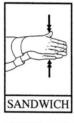 SANDWICH

 SAUSAGES

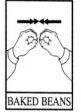 BAKED BEANS

 TOAST

 PASTIE

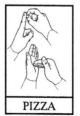 PIZZA

 SOUP

CHEW	EAT	DINNER	BEEFBURGER
CHOP	FISH FINGER	PIE	CHIPS
SPAGHETTI	MEAT	ROAST	BEEF
GRAVY	KETCHUP	SAUCE	SALT

FOOD AND DRINK

PARTY

PICNIC

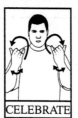

CELEBRATE

RECIPE

FLOUR

CAKE

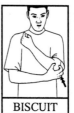

BISCUIT

CRISPS

ICE CREAM

LOLLIPOP

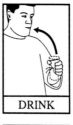

DRINK

BEER

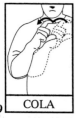

COLA

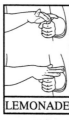

LEMONADE

ORANGE JUICE

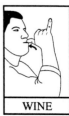

WINE

FRUIT

APPLE

BANANA

CHERRY

GRAPE

GRAPEFRUIT

LEMON

PEACH

PEAR

PINEAPPLE

PLUM

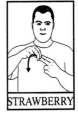
STRAWBERRY

NUT

COCONUT

BERRY

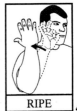
RIPE

VEGETABLES

BEAN

CABBAGE

CARROT

CAULIFLOWER

MUSHROOM

PEAS

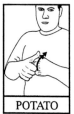

POTATO

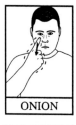

ONION

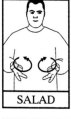

SALAD

BEETROOT

CUCUMBER

LETTUCE

TOMATO

SPROUTS

SWEDE (turnip)

 TEA	 COFFEE	 MILK	CREAM (milk)
SUGAR	CHOCOLATE	RICE	PUDDING
CUSTARD	JELLY	JAM	YOGURT
CAN (drink)	SEAFOOD	BACON	VINEGAR

42

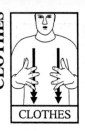

CLOTHES

BRA

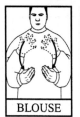

BLOUSE

DRESS

SKIRT

STOCKING

SANDAL

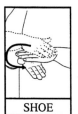

SHOE

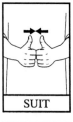

SUIT

ANORAK

JEANS

JUMPER

COAT

MITTEN

RAINCOAT

SCARF

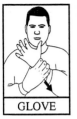			
GLOVE	HAT	VEST	T-SHIRT
		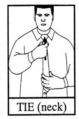	
BUTTONS	SHIRT	TIE (neck)	TROUSERS
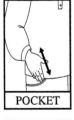	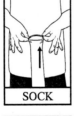		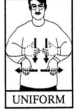
POCKET	SOCK	BOOT	UNIFORM
	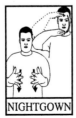	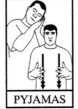	
DRESSING GOWN	NIGHTGOWN	PYJAMAS	SLIPPER

ANIMALS	HERD	ELEPHANT

DONKEY

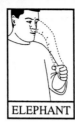

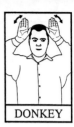

CAMEL	LEOPARD	LION	TIGER

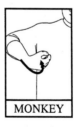

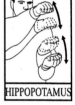

BEAR	GORILLA	MONKEY	HIPPOPOTAMUS

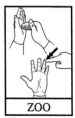

RHINOCEROS	GIRAFFE	CROCODILE	ZOO

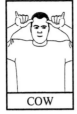			
BULL	COW	PIG	GOAT
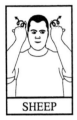	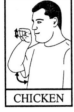		
SHEEP	CHICKEN	DUCK	GOOSE

HEN	TURKEY	DEER	HARE

SQUIRREL	FOX	WOLF	WORM

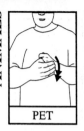

PET

HORSE

DOG

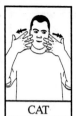

CAT

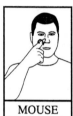

MOUSE

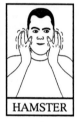

HAMSTER

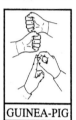

GUINEA-PIG

RABBIT

TORTOISE

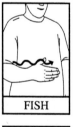

FISH

GOLDFISH

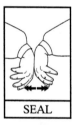

SEAL

SNAKE

BIRD

BUDGIE

OWL

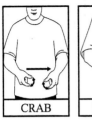	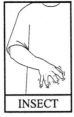		
CRAB	INSECT	FLY	CATERPILLAR
	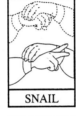	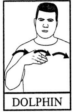	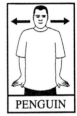
BUTTERFLY	SNAIL	DOLPHIN	PENGUIN
	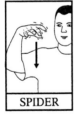	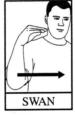	
FROG	SPIDER	SWAN	ZEBRA

WHALE	PARROT	KANGAROO	SHARK

COUNTRY

AMERICA

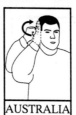

AUSTRALIA

AUSTRIA

AFRICA

BRITAIN

CHINA

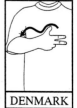

DENMARK

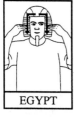

EGYPT

FRANCE

GERMANY

GREECE

HOLLAND

IRELAND

INDIA

ITALY

		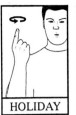	
EUROPE	TOUR	HOLIDAY	ABROAD
	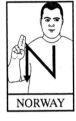		
JAPAN	NORWAY	RUSSIA	SCOTLAND

SPAIN	SWEDEN	SWITZERLAND	WORLD
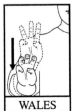		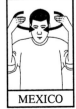	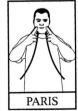
WALES	CANADA	MEXICO	PARIS

LONDON

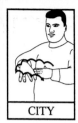

CITY

TOWN

MARKET

VALLEY

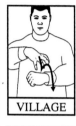

VILLAGE

FARM

LAKE

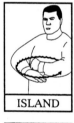

ISLAND

ROCK

PIER

COAST

BEACH

SAND

SEA

HOTEL

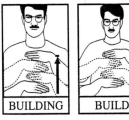

BUILDING | BUILD

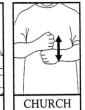

CHURCH

CASTLE

STATION

RAILWAY

LIBRARY

SCHOOL

BANK

HOSPITAL

THEATRE

CINEMA

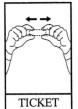

TICKET

PRIVATE

LAND

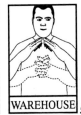

WAREHOUSE

BUSINESS	EMPLOYER	JOB	OFFICE
INTERVIEW	SHIFT (work)	FACTORY	EARN
WAGES	OFF (absent)	SACK	RESIGN
PAY	UNEMPLOYED	DOLE	CLAIM

BANK	DEPOSIT	BORROW	OWE
	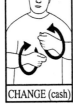		
CHEQUE	CHANGE (cash)	PENNY / PENCE	POUND
			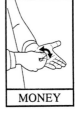
COIN	COUNTER	COUNT	MONEY
		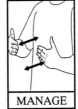	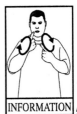
SAVE	TOTAL	MANAGE	INFORMATION

BANK AND SHOPS

SHOPPING

SHOP

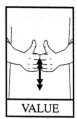
VALUE

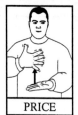
PRICE

CHARGE (price)

CHEAP

EXPENSIVE

BUY

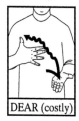
DEAR (costly)

SPEND

CHANGE (cash)

LIST

PROFIT

WORTH

CARRY

BAG

NEWSPAPER

CAMPAIGN

ADVERTISE

NEWS

PRINT

DISTRIBUTE

POST OFFICE

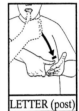
LETTER (post)

CORRESPOND

PUBLISHED

LETTER (abc)

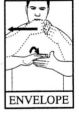
ENVELOPE

STAMP (post)

POST

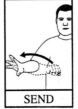
SEND

REPLY

HOSPITAL	DOCTOR	NURSE	HURT
ILL	BLOOD	OPERATION	BANDAGE
NEEDLE	INJECT	X-RAY	HEART
MEDICINE	TABLET	DIZZY	REST

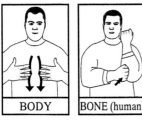

BODY

BONE (human)

PREGNANT

BABY

BORN

SICK

FAINT

POORLY

COUGH

COLD (flu)

SPOTS

PILL

DEPRESSED

HEALTH

THERMOMETER

WHEELCHAIR

58

NAME

ADDRESS

AGE

APPOINTMENT

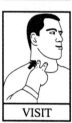

VISIT

FALL

PAIN

POISON

BLIND

DISABLED

HANDICAP

TEST

WEIGH

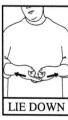

LIE DOWN

TIRED

SLEEP

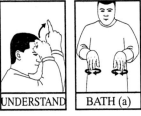

UNDERSTAND	BATH (a)

SHOWER	HOT

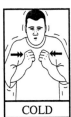

COLD	SOAP	TOWEL	WASH

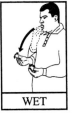
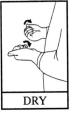

FEEL	WET	DRY	CREAM (medicine)

SEW	TOILET	DARK	LIGHT (dark)

WAKE UP	DREAM	TOSS AND TURN	ASLEEP
AWAKE	COMFORT	COMFORTABLE	FIT (healthy)
WELL	NURSERY	COOL	WARM
SPECIAL	MACHINE	DEAD	LIVE

SPORT

BAT

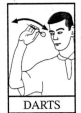

BALL

DARTS

FOOTBALL

MATCH

GOAL

SCORE

COMPETITION

LOST

WIN

PRIZE (trophy)

GAME

CRICKET

RUGBY

SNOOKER

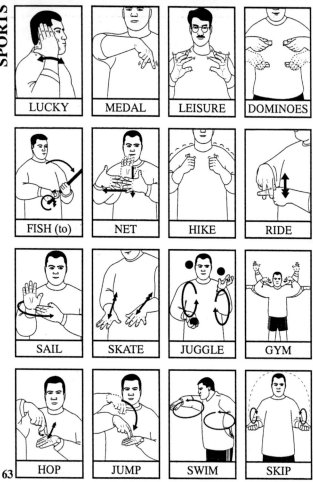

LUCKY	MEDAL	LEISURE	DOMINOES
FISH (to)	NET	HIKE	RIDE
SAIL	SKATE	JUGGLE	GYM
HOP	JUMP	SWIM	SKIP

GOD

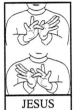

HEAVEN

JESUS

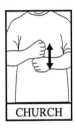

LORD

CHURCH

BISHOP

PRIEST

NUN

CATHOLIC

PROTESTANT

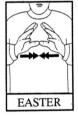

CHRISTMAS

EASTER

CROSS

SING

SONG

PRAY

MARRY	BRIDE	BLESS	ANGEL
HOLY	CRUCIFY	FORGIVE	BELL
SOUL	PRAISE	SHEPHERD	SUNDAY
COLLECTION	KNEEL	WEDDING	CHRISTENING

DETECTIVE

POLICE

ARREST

CHARGE (law)

LAW

COURT (law)

JUDGE

OATH

DOUBT

DEFEND

STEAL

KILL

FINE (pay)

HANG

PRISON

ESCAPE

FORCE

CATCH

TROUBLE

SUSPICIOUS

TRUE

FALSE

TRUTH

LIE (untrue)

THIEVE

PROOF

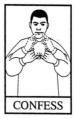

CONFESS

REPRESENT

SHAME (guilt)

MERCY

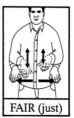

FAIR (just)

FREE (to)

AMBULANCE

FIRE ENGINE

POLICE CAR

BUS

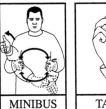

MINIBUS

TAXI

CAR

CARAVAN

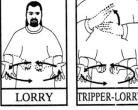

LORRY

TRIPPER-LORRY

MOTORBIKE

BICYCLE

TRACTOR

TRAIN

UNDERGROUND TRAIN

AEROPLANE

TRANSPORT	DRIVE	TRAFFIC	ACCIDENT

AHEAD	DANGER	WARN	SIGN (warning)
	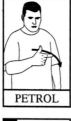		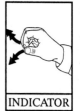
GARAGE	PETROL	HEADLIGHTS	INDICATOR

FORWARD	REVERSE	NUMBER	PLATE (car)

 TRAFFIC LIGHTS	LAMP	SINGLE (one)	 LINE
 BACK	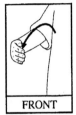 FRONT	 FOR	 HIRE
 ALARM	 INSURE	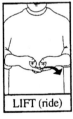 LIFT (ride)	 PAVEMENT
 SEEM	 SITUATION	 CONCENTRATE	 SKILL

CRASH

FAULT

MISTAKE

SERIOUS

DISTANCE

JOURNEY

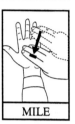

MILE

TRAVEL

STRAIGHT

THROUGH

TURN

CORNER

KEEP

CLEAR

EAST

WEST

HILL	START	FAST	SLOW
MIDDLE	SIDE	BUSY	ROAD
APPROACH	GO	STOP	PARK (car)
OVERTAKE	FOG	FAIL	PASS

CONFIDENT

PRACTICE

UNDERSTAND

MIRROR

GEAR

MOVE

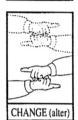

CHANGE (alter)

FOLLOW (car)

ACROSS

DOUBLE

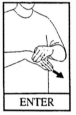

ENTER

SLIP

DELAY

HALT

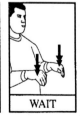

WAIT

MAXIMUM

		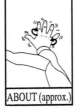	
A	ABOUT (concerning)	ABOUT (approx.)	ABOUT (the area)
	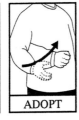		
ACTUAL	ADOPT	ADVANTAGE	AGAINST (versus)

AGAIN	AIM	AIR	ALL
			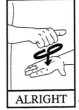
ALL THE TIME	ALLOW	ALONE	ALRIGHT

ALSO

ALREADY

ALTERNATE

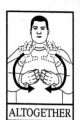
ALTOGETHER

ALWAYS

AMAZE

ANNOUNCE

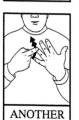
ANOTHER

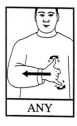
ANY

ANYWHERE

APOLOGISE

APPOINT

APPROVE

ARGUE

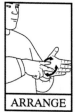
ARRANGE

ATTITUDE

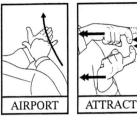 AIRPORT

 ATTRACT

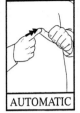 AUTOMATIC

 AWAY

 BACKWARDS

 BAKING

 BALANCE

 BALLOON

 BARE

 BASIC

 BATH (to)

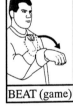 BEAT (game)

 BECAUSE

 BECOME

 BEHAVE

 BEHIND

 BELONG

 BELT

 BESIDE

 BET

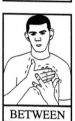 BETWEEN

 BIRTHDAY

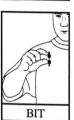 BIT

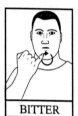 BITTER

 BLAME

 BLANK

 BLONDE

 BLUSH

 BOAST

 BOIL

 BONUS

 BORED

BOAT

BOSS

BOTH

BOX

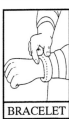

BRACELET

BREAK

BRIGHT

BRUSH (a)

BRUSH (to)

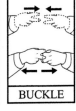

BUCKLE

BULLY

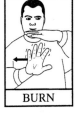

BURN

BURST

BURY

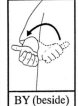

BY (beside)

BY (past)

CALM DOWN

CAMP

CAMERA

CANCEL

CANDLE

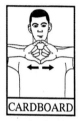
CARDBOARD

CARPENTRY

CEMENT MIXER

CENTRE

CHAIN

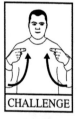
CHALLENGE

CHASE

CHEAT

CHECK

CHEEKY

CHOOSE

79

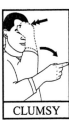

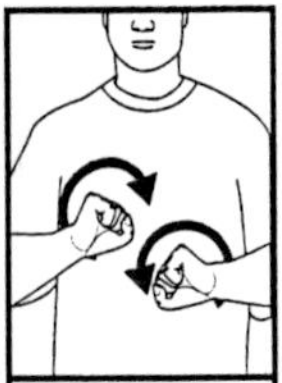
CLEAN (to)

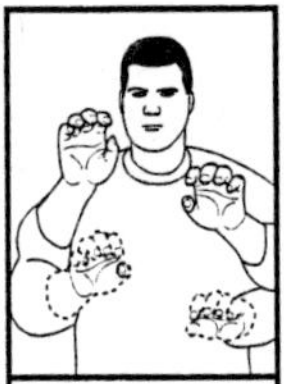
CLIMB

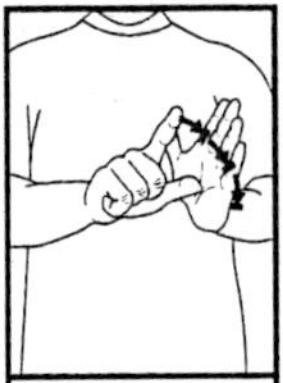
CLOCK

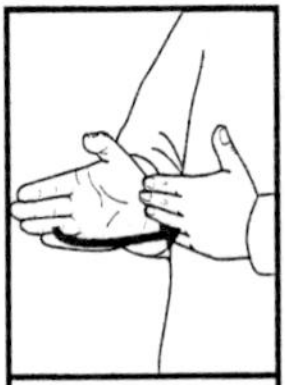
CLOSE (door)

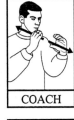

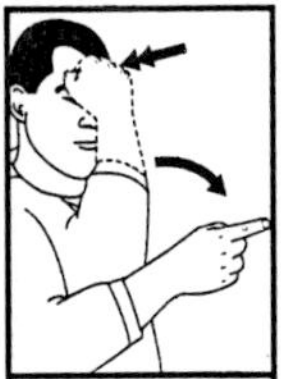
CLUMSY

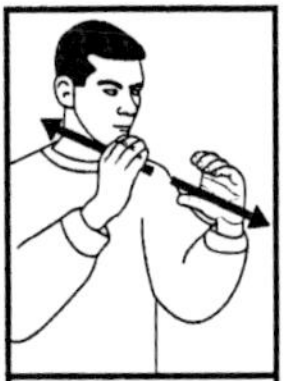
COACH

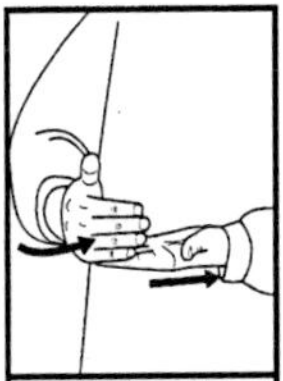
COLLECT

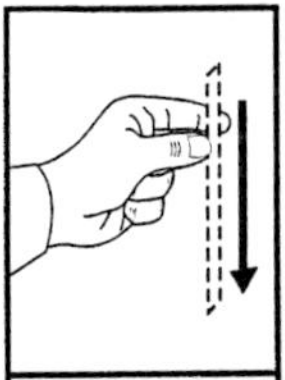
COLUMN

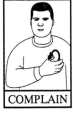

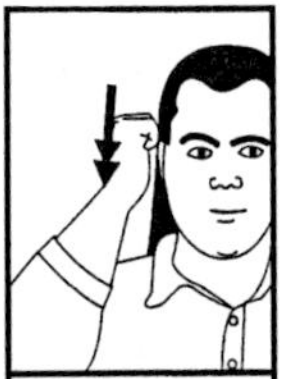
COMB

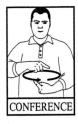

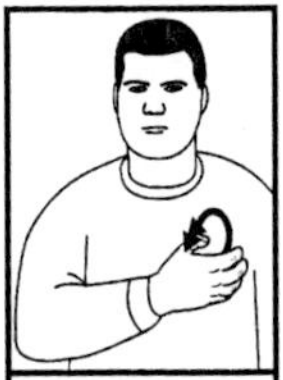
COMPLAIN

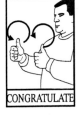

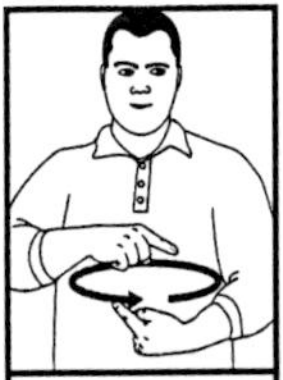
CONFERENCE

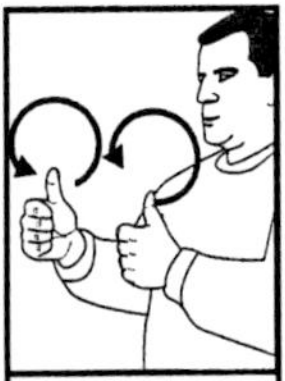
CONGRATULATE

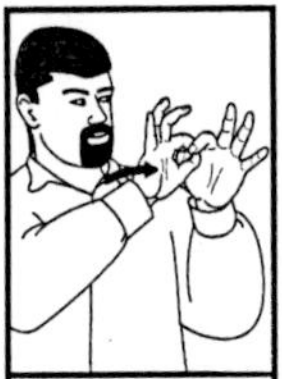
CONTACT

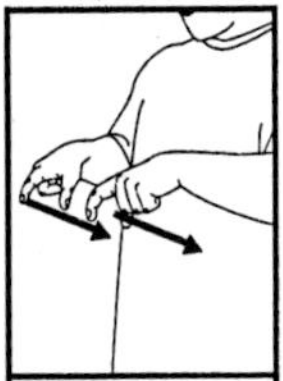
CONTINUE

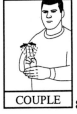

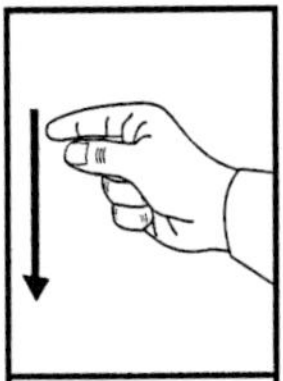
COST

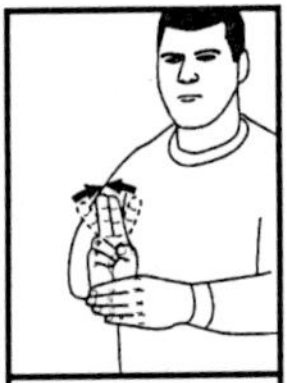
COUPLE

COURAGE

COURSE

CRANE

CRITICISE

CROWD

CROWDED

CROWN

CRUSH

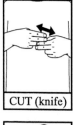
CUT (knife)

CUT (scissors)

DAMAGE

DAMP

DECIDE / DECISION

DEJECTED

DESIGN

DELIBERATE

		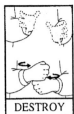	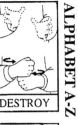
DEMAND	DEPEND	DESCRIBE	DESTROY
	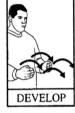		
DETERMINED	DEVELOP	DICTIONARY	DIFFICULT
			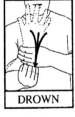
DISAPPEAR	DISAPPOINT	DROP	DROWN
			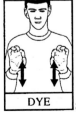
DRUNK	DUCK (to)	DURING	DYE

82

EARRINGS

EDGE

EITHER

ELASTIC

ELSE

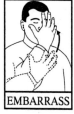
EMBARRASS

ENCOURAGE

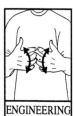
ENGINEERING

ENJOY

ENOUGH

EQUAL

ESTABLISH

ESTIMATE

EVEN

EVENTUALLY

EXACT

EXAMPLE (e.g.)

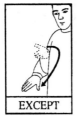
EXCEPT

EXCHANGE

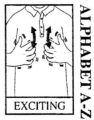
EXCITING

EXCUSE

EXPECT

EXPERIENCE

EXPLAIN

EXTRA

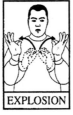
EXPLOSION

EXIT

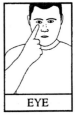
EYE

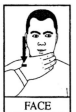
FACE

FAKE

FANCY

FASHION

84

FAMOUS

FASCINATE

FAVOUR

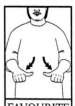

FAVOURITE

FEATHER

FED UP

FEED

FIGHT

FILL

FINGERPRINT

FIT (together)

FIX (fasten)

FIX (mend)

FLAG

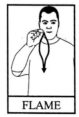

FLAME

FLAT

		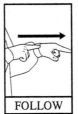	
FLOAT	FOLD	FOLLOW	FOOD

FOOL	FOREVER	FREE	FREEDOM
		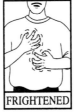	
FRESH	FREEZE	FRIGHTENED	FROZEN
	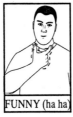		
FUNERAL	FUNNY (ha ha)	FUNNY (odd)	FUTURE

GENERAL

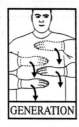

GENERATION

GHOST

GLASSES

GLUE

GOSSIP

GOVERNMENT

GREASE

GREEDY

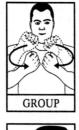

GROUP

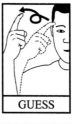

GUESS

GUIDE

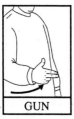

GUN

GYPSY

GONE

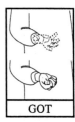

GOT

HAIR	HAMMER	HEIGHT	HELICOPTER

HEREDITARY	HIDE	HOLD	HOLE

   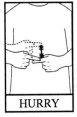

HONOUR	HOW OLD	HUNGRY	HURRY

 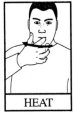  

HONEST	HEAT	HISTORY	HOOVER

IDEA

IGNORE

IMAGINE

IMPORTANT

IMPRESSED

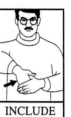

IMPROVE

INCLUDE

INSTEAD

INTEGRATE

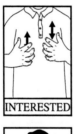

INTERESTED

INTERRUPT

INJURY

INTO

INTRODUCE

JEALOUS

JOIN

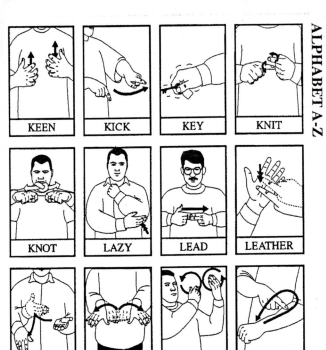

KEEN	KICK	KEY	KNIT
KNOT	LAZY	LEAD	LEATHER
LEFT (over)	LIKE (similar)	LONG TIME AGO	LONG (time)

LONELY	LOOK AFTER	LOOK	LOVELY

MAGAZINE

MAGIC

MAKE

MANNERS

MANY

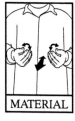
MATERIAL

MATTER (the)

MEAN (imply)

MEET

MEETING

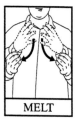
MELT

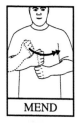
MEND

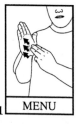
MENU

METAL

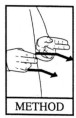
METHOD

MISS

			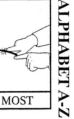
MISERABLE	MIX	MOODY	MOST

MOUNTAIN	NAUGHTY	NEARLY	NEED

NEIGHBOUR	NERVOUS	NEVER	NEXT

NO (not any)	NONE	NOT	NOT YET

OBJECT (to)

O'CLOCK

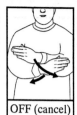
OFF (cancel)

ONCE

ONLY

OPPORTUNITY

OPPOSE

OPPOSITE (idea)

OPPOSITE (place)

ORAL

ORDER (arrange)

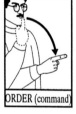
ORDER (command)

ORGANISE

OTHER

OTHERS

OR

93

PACK

PAINT

PAIR

PANIC

PARALLEL

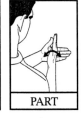
PART

PARTICULAR

PAST (the)

PATTERN

PERFECT

PERSUADE

PHOTO

PIPE

PLACE

PLAN

PLASTIC

PLENTY

POEM

POINT (make a)

POPULAR

POSH

POWER

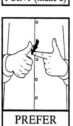

PREFER

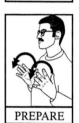

PREPARE

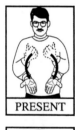

PRESENT

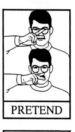

PRETEND

PROBLEM

PROFESSION

PROMISE

PUBLICITY

PUPPET (string)

PUT

QUARREL

QUEUE

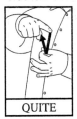
QUITE

RAFFLE

RAINBOW

RAISE

RATHER

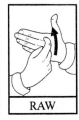
RAW

READY

REAL / REALLY

REASON

RECENTLY

RECOGNISE

REFRACTION

REFUSE

REGISTER

REGULAR	RELATE	RELEASE	RENT

REPEAT	RESEARCH	RESPONSIBILITY	REVENGE

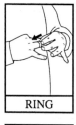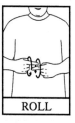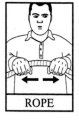

RING	RISK	ROLL	ROPE

RUBBISH	RUDE (indecent)	RULES	RUSH

 SAFE	SATISFIED	SCARE	SCREW
SEARCH	SECOND (2nd)	SECRET	SELFISH
SERIES	SHADE	SHAME (pity)	SHARE
SHARP	SHAVE	SHINE	STOCK

98

SHORTS

SHOW

SHY

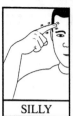

SILLY

SIMILAR

SINCE

SLY

SMACK

SMART

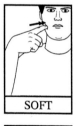

SOFT

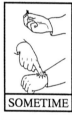

SOMETIME

SOON

SORRY

SORT OUT

SPACE

SPILL

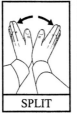 SPIT

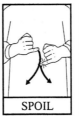 SPLIT

 SPOIL

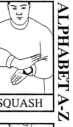 SQUASH

 STEEL

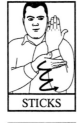 STICKS

 STILL

 STOMACH

 STOP

 STRIKE (on)

 STRING

 STUCK

 STUPID

 SUNRISE

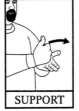 SUPPORT

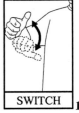 SWITCH

| TAIL | TAKE IN (absorb) | TALE | TALL |

 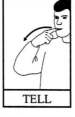  

| TEMPT | TELL | TEAR (rip) | TEASE |

 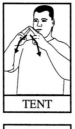  

| TEMPORARY | TENT | THEORY | THOROUGH |

  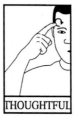 

| THROW | THROAT | THOUGHTFUL | THREAD |

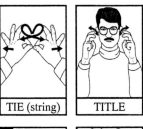			
TIE (string)	TITLE	TOE	TOIL
	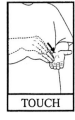		
TORMENT	TOUCH	TOWARDS	TREBLE (3x)
			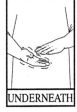
TRIP	TRUST	TWICE	UNDERNEATH
	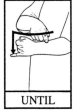		
UNLESS	UNTIL	UPSET	USE

VARIOUS

VOCABULARY

VOTE

WAR

WASTE

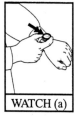

WATCH (a)

WATCH (to)

WATER

WAVE

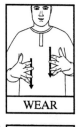

WEAR

WEED

WELCOME

WHILE

WHISPER

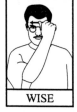

WISE

WISH

 WHISTLE

 WING

 WILD

 WIPE

 WIRE

 WITCH

 WITHDRAW

 WITNESS

 WONDERFUL

 WOOD

 WOOL

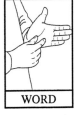 WORD

 WORRY

 WOULD

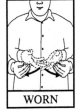 WORN

 WHAT TIME ?

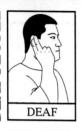	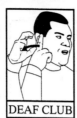		
DEAF	DEAF CLUB	QUIET	SILENT
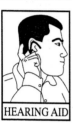			
HEARING AID	EARMOULD	HEARING	HEAR
	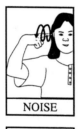	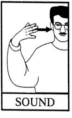	
LISTEN	NOISE	SOUND	VOICE

SHOUT	SPEAK	TALK	CONVERSATION

TELEPHONE

CALL

LISTEN

SPEAK

HELP

NUMBER

FOR

AMBULANCE

FIRE

POLICE

9 9 9

DEAF

COMMUNICATE

VOICE

MINICOM

106

INDEX

A

A 74
ABOUT (approx.) 74
ABOUT (concerning) 74
ABOUT (area) 74
ABOVE 17
ABROAD 50
ACCIDENT 69
ACROSS 73
ACT 27
ACTUAL 74
ADD 24
ADDRESS 59
ADOPT 74
ADULT 20
ADVANTAGE 74
ADVERTISE 56
AEROPLANE 68
AFRICAN 49
AFTER 9
AFTERNOON 28
AGAIN 74
AGAINST (vs) 74
AGE 59
AGREE 17
AHEAD 69
AIM 74
AIR 74
AIRPORT 76
ALARM 70
ALL 74
ALL THE TIME 74
ALLOW 74
ALONE 74
ALPHABET 24
ALREADY 75
ALRIGHT 74
ALSO 75
ALTERNATE 75
ALTOGETHER 75
ALWAYS 75
AMAZE 75
AMBULANCE .... 68 & 106
AMERICA 49
AND 7
ANGEL 65
ANGLE 25
ANGRY 17
ANIMAL 45
ANORAK 43
ANOTHER 74
ANNOUNCE 75

ANSWER 26
ANY 75
ANYWHERE 75
APOLOGISE 75
APPLE 40
APPOINT 75
APPOINTMENT 59
APPRENTICE 22
APPROACH 72
APPROVE 75
ARE 8
ARGUE 75
ARITHMETIC 25
ARMCHAIR 32
ARMY 20
ARRANGE 75
ARREST 66
ARRIVE 13
ART 25
ASK 26
ASLEEP 61
ATTITUDE 75
ATTRACT 76
AUNTIE 19
AUSTRALIA 49
AUSTRIA 49
AUTOMATIC 76
AUTUMN 30
AWAKE 61
AWAY 76
AWFUL 18

B

BABY 58
BABY-SIT 36
BACK 70
BACKWARDS 76
BACON 42
BAD 12
BAG 55
BAKE 34
BAKE BEAN 37
BAKING 76
BALANCE 76
BALL 62
BALLOON 62
BANANA 40
BANDAGE 57
BANK .... 52 & 54
BARE 76
BASIC 76
BAT 62
BATH (a) 60

BATH (to) 76
BEACH 51
BEAN 41
BEAR 45
BEAT 76
BEAUTIFUL 18
BECAUSE 76
BECOME 76
BED 32
BEEF 38
BEEFBURGER 38
BEEN 13
BEER 39
BEETROOT 41
BEFORE (past) 9
BEFORE 9
BEGIN 17
BEHAVE 76
BEHIND 76
BELIEVE 12
BELL 65
BELONG 77
BELOW 17
BELT 44
BERRY 40
BEST 16
BESIDE 77
BET 77
BETTER 16
BETWEEN 77
BICYCLE 68
BIG 18
BIRD 47
BIRTHDAY 77
BISCUIT 39
BISHOP 64
BIT 77
BITTER 77
BLACK 4
BLAME 77
BLANK 77
BLANKET 32
BLESS 65
BLIND 77
BLONDE 4
BLOOD 57
BLOUSE 43
BLUE 4
BLUSH 77
BOAST 77
BOAT 68
BODY 58
BOIL 77
BONE (human) 58

BONUS 77
BOOK 23
BOOT 44
BORED 77
BORN 58
BORROW 54
BOSS 78
BOTH 78
BOTTLE 5
BOTTOM 10
BOUNCER 21
BOWL 34
BOX 78
BOY 4
BRA 43
BRACELET 44
BRITAIN 49
BRANCH 35
BREAD 78
BREAK 78
BREAKFAST 37
BRICK 31
BRIDE 65
BRIGHT 78
BRING 4
BRONZE 3
BROTHER 19
BROWN 4
BRUSH (a) 78
BRUSH (to) 78
BUCKLE 78
BUDGIE 47
BUILDING 52
BUILD 52
BULB 31
BULL 46
BULLY 37
BUN 37
BUNK BED 32
BURN 78
BURST 78
BURY 78
BUS 68
BUSH 35
BUSINESS 53
BUSY 78
BUT 9
BUTCHER 22
BUTTER 37
BUTTERFLY 48
BUTTON 44
BUY 55
BY (beside) 78
BY (past) 78

C

CABBAGE	41
CAKE	39
CALENDAR	28
CALL	106
CALM DOWN	79
CAMEL	45
CAMERA	79
CAMP	79
CAMPAIGN	56
CAN	9
CAN (drink)	42
CANADA	50
CARDBOARD	79
CANCEL	79
CANDLE	79
CAN'T	9
CAR	68
CARAVAN	68
CARE	12
CAREFUL	12
CARELESS	12
CARPET	32
CARPENTRY	79
CARROT	41
CARRY	55
CASTLE	52
CAT	47
CATCH	67
CATHOLIC	64
CATERPILLAR	48
CAULIFLOWER	41
CEILING	31
CELEBRATE	39
CEMENT MIXER	79
CENTRE	79
CHAIN	79
CHAIR	32
CHAIRPERSON	21
CHALLENGE	79
CHANGE (cash)	54 & 55
CHANGE (alter)	73
CHARGE (price)	55
CHARGE (law)	66
CHASE	79
CHEAP	79
CHEAT	79
CHECK	79
CHEEKY	79
CHEESE	37
CHEQUE	54
CHERRY	40

CHEW	38
CHICKEN	46
CHILD	20
CHILDREN	19
CHIMNEY	31
CHINA	49
CHIPS	38
CHOCOLATE	42
CHOOSE	79
CHOP	38
CHRISTENING	65
CHRISTMAS	64
CHURCH	52 & 64
CINEMA	52
CITY	51
CLAIM	53
CLASS	23
CLEAN	16
CLEAN (to)	80
CLEAR	71
CLEVER	26
CLIMB	79
CLOCK	80
CLOSE	80
CLOTHES	43
CLOUDS	29
CLUMSY	80
COACH	80
COAST	51
COAT	43
COCONUT	40
COFFEE	42
COIN	54
COLA	42
COLD (flu)	58
COLD	60
COLLECT	80
COLLECTION	65
COLLEGE	26
COLOUR	4
COLUMN	80
COMB	80
COME	13
COMFORT	61
COMFORTABLE	61
COMMITTEE	21
COMMUNICATE .. 26 & 106
COMPETITION	62
COMPLAIN	80
COMPUTER	27
CONCENTRATE	70
CONFERENCE	80
CONFESS	67
CONFIDENT	73

CONGRATULATE	80
CONCENTRATE	70
CONTACT	80
CONTINUE	80
COOK	34
COOL	61
COOKER	33
CORNER	71
CORNFLAKES	37
CORRESPOND	56
COST	80
COUGH	58
COUNT	54
COUNTER	54
COUNTRY	49
COUPLE	80
COURAGE	81
COURSE	81
COURT	66
COUSIN	19
COW	46
CRAB	48
CRANE	81
CRASH	71
CREAM (colour)	4
CREAM (milk)	42
CREAM (medicine)	60
CRICKET	62
CRITICISE	81
CRISPS	39
CROCODILE	45
CROSS	64
CRUCIFY	65
CRUEL	14
CROWD	81
CROWDED	81
CROWN	81
CRUSH	81
CRY	18
CUCUMBER	41
CUP	33
CUPBOARD	33
CURRICULUM	23
CURTAIN	32
CURVE	25
CUSTARD	37
CUT (knife)	81
CUT (scissors)	81

D

DAMAGE	81
DAMP	81
DANCE	27

DANGER	69
DARK	60
DARTS	62
DATE	28
DAUGHTER	19
DAY	28
DEAD	61
DEAF	105 & 106
DEAF CLUB	105
DEAR	55
DECIDE/DECISION	81
DECREASE	11
DEEP	11
DEER	46
DEFEND	66
DEJECTED	81
DELAY	73
DELIBERATE	81
DENMARK	49
DEMAND	82
DEPOSIT	54
DEPEND	82
DEPRESSED	58
DESCRIBE	82
DESIGN	81
DESTROY	82
DETECTIVE	66
DETERMINED	82
DEVELOP	82
DISAPPEAR	82
DICTIONARY	82
DIFFERENT	11
DIFFICULT	82
DINNER	38
DIRTY	16
DISABLED	59
DISAGREE	17
DISAPPOINT	82
DISH	34
DISTRIBUTE	56
DISTANCE	71
DIVIDEND	24
DIVORCE	21
DIZZY	57
DO	9
DOCTOR	57
DOG	47
DOLE	53
DOLPHIN	48
DOMINOES	63
DONKEY	45
DON'T	9
DON'T BELIEVE	12
DON'T CARE	12

108

INDEX

DON'T KNOW 6
DON'T LIKE 9
DON'T WANT 5
DOOR 31
DOUBLE 73
DOUBT 66
DOWN 17
DRAWERS 33
DREAM 61
DRESS 43
DRESSING GOWN 44
DRESSING TABLE 32
DRINK 39
DRIVE 69
DROP 82
DROWN 82
DRUM 27
DRUNK 82
DRY 60
DUCK (bird) 46
DUCK (to) 82
DURING 82
DYE 82

E

EACH 8
EARLY 10
EARMOULD 105
EARN 53
EARRING 85
EAST 71
EASTER 64
EASY 10
EAT 38
EDGE 83
EDUCATION 23
EGG 37
EGYPT 49
EIGHT 2
EIGHTEEN 2
EIGHTY 3
EITHER 83
ELASTIC 83
ELECTRIC 33
ELEPHANT 45
ELEVEN 2
ELSE 83
EMBARRASS 83
EMPLOYER 53
EMPTY 15
ENCOURAGE 83
END 17
ENGAGED 21

ENGINEERING 83
ENGLISH 24
ENJOY 83
ENOUGH 83
ENTER 73
ENVELOPE 56
EQUAL 83
ESCAPE 66
ESTABLISH 83
ESTIMATE 83
EUROPE 50
EVEN 83
EVENING 29
EVENTUALLY 83
EVER 8
EVERY 8
EVERYDAY 28
EVERYONE 14
EVERYTHING 16
EXACT 83
EXAM 26
EXAMPLE (e.g.) 84
EXCEPT 84
EXCHANGER 84
EXCITING (interest) 84
EXCUSE 84
EXIT 84
EXPECT 84
EXPENSIVE 55
EXPERIENCE 84
EXPLAIN 84
EXPLOSION 84
EXTRA 84
EYE 84

F

FACE 84
FACTORY 53
FAIL 72
FAINT 58
FAIR (just) 67
FAKE 84
FALL 59
FALSE 67
FAMILY 19
FAMOUS 85
FANCY 84
FAR 13
FARM 51
FARMER 22
FASCINATE 85
FASHION 84
FAST .... 10 & 72

FAT 16
FATHER 19
FAULT 71
FAVOUR 85
FAVOURITE 85
FEATHER 85
FED UP 85
FEED 85
FEEL 60
FENCE 35
FEW 15
FIELD 35
FIFTEEN 2
FIFTY 3
FIGHT 85
FILL 85
FILM 27
FIND 14
FINE (pay) 66
FINGERPRINT 85
FINGER SPELL 26
FINISH 17
FIRE 106
FIRE ENGINE 68
FIREMAN 22
FIREPLACE 32
FISH (a) 47
FISH (to) 63
FISH FINGER 38
FIT (healthy) 61
FIT (together) 85
FIVE 2
FIX (fasten) 85
FIX (mend) 85
FLAG 85
FLAME 85
FLAT 85
FLOAT 86
FLOUR 39
FLOWER 35
FLY 48
FOG .... 30 & 72
FOLD 86
FOLLOW 86
FOLLOW (car) 73
FOOD 86
FOOL 86
FOOTBALL 62
FOR .... 70 & 106
FORCE 86
FOREMAN 22
FOREST 36
FOREVER 85
FORGOT 14

FORGIVE 65
FORK 34
FORTNIGHT 29
FORWARD 69
FORTY 3
FOUR 2
FOURTEEN 2
FOX 46
FRACTION 25
FRANCE 49
FREE (to) 67
FREEDOM 86
FREE 86
FREEZE 86
FRESH 86
FRIEND 20
FRIDGE 33
FRIGHTENED 86
FROG 48
FROM 13
FRONT 70
FROST 30
FROZEN 86
FRUIT 40
FRY 34
FULL 15
FUNERAL 86
FUNNY (ha ha) 86
FUNNY (odd) 86
FURNITURE 32
FUTURE 86

G

GALE 30
GAME 62
GARAGE 69
GARDEN 35
GAS 33
GATE 35
GEAR 73
GENERAL 87
GENERATION 87
GENEROUS 14
GERMANY 49
GET 8
GHOST 87
GIRAFFE 45
GIRL 20
GIVE 13
GLASS 31
GLASS (drink) 34
GLASSES 87
GLOVE 44

GLUE 87
GO .... 13 & 72
GOAL 62
GOAT 46
GOD 64
GOLD 4
GOLDFISH 47
GONE 87
GOOD 12
GOODBYE 12
GOOD MORNING 28
GORILLA 45
GOOSE 46
GOSSIP 87
GOT 87
GOVERNMENT 87
GRANDFATHER 19
GRAMMAR 25
GRANDMOTHER 19
GRAPE 40
GRAPEFRUIT 40
GRASS 35
GRAVY 38
GREASE 87
GREECE 49
GREEDY 87
GREEN 4
GREY 4
GRILL 34
GROUP 87
GROW 35
GUESS 87
GUIDE (lead) 87
GUINEA-PIG 47
GUN 87
GUITAR 27
GYM 63
GYPSY 87

H

HAIR 88
HALF 25
HALL 31
HALT 73
HAMMER 88
HAMSTER 47
HANDICAP 59
HANDLE 31
HANDSOME 18
HANG 66
HAPPEN 11
HAPPY 12
HARD 10

HARE 46
HAT 44
HATE 18
HAVE 6
HE 21
HEADLIGHTS 69
HEADMASTER 23
HEALTH 58
HEAT 88
HEAR 105
HEARING 105
HEARING AID 105
HEART 57
HEAVEN 57
HEAVY 14
HEDGE 35
HEIGHT 88
HELLO 12
HELP 106
HELICOPTER 88
HEN 46
HER (posses.) 7
HER (indic.) 7
HERD 45
HERE 8
HEREDITARY 88
HIDE 88
HIDE 88
HIGH 10
HIGHCHAIR 36
HIKE 63
HILL 72
HIM 21
HIPPOPOTAMUS 45
HIRE 70
HIS 7
HISTORY 88
HOLD 88
HOLE 88
HOLIDAY 50
HOLLAND 49
HOLY 65
HOME 31
HONEST 88
HONOUR 88
HOOVER 88
HOP 63
HORSE 47
HOSPITAL .... 52 & 57
HOT 60
HOTDOG 37
HOTEL 51
HOUR 28
HOUSE 31
HOW 5

HOW OLD 88
HUNDRED .... 3 & 25
HUNGRY 88
HURRY 88
HURT 57
HUSBAND 20

I

I 7
ICE 30
ICE CREAM 39
IDEA 89
IF 8
IGNORE 89
INJURY 89
ILL 57
IMAGINE 89
IMPRESSED 89
IMPORTANT 89
IMPOSSIBLE 15
IMPROVE 89
IN 9
INCLUDE 89
INCREASE 11
INDIA 49
INDICATOR 69
INFORMATION 54
INTO 89
INJECT 57
IS 8
INSECT 48
INSTEAD 89
INSIDE 11
INSURE 70
INTEGRATE 89
INTERPRET 26
INTERESTED 89
INTRODUCE 89
INTERRUPT 89
INTERVIEW 53
IRELAND 49
IRON 34
ISLAND 51
ITALY 49

J

JAM 42
JAPAN 50
JAR 34
JEALOUS 89
JEANS 43
JELLY 42

JESUS 64
JIGSAW 36
JOB 53
JOIN 89
JOKE 18
JUDGE 66
JOURNEY 71
JUG 33
JUGGLE 63
JUMP 63
JUMPER 43
JUST 12

K

KANGAROO 48
KEEN 90
KEEP 71
KETCHUP 38
KETTLE 33
KEY 90
KICK 90
KILL 66
KIND (good) 14
KING 22
KITCHEN 31
KITE 36
KNEEL 65
KNIFE 34
KNIGHT 22
KNIT 90
KNOT 90
KNOW 6

L

LAKE 51
LAMP 70
LAND 52
LANGUAGE 26
LAST NIGHT 28
LAST WEEK 29
LAST YEAR 29
LATE 10
LATER 9
LAUGH 18
LAW 66
LAZY 90
LEAD 90
LEAF 35
LEARN 23
LEATHER 90
LEAVE 13
LECTURE 26

110

INDEX

LEFT (over) 90
LEISURE 63
LEMON 40
LEMONADE 39
LEOPARD 45
LESS 15
LESSON 23
LETTER (post) 56
LETTER (abc) 56
LETTUCE 41
LIBRARY 52
LID 34
LIE (untrue) 67
LIE DOWN 59
LIFT (ride) 70
LIGHT (dark) 60
LIGHT (weight) 14
LIGHTNING 30
LIKE 9
LIKE (similar) 90
LINE 70
LION 45
LIST 55
LISTEN .... 105 & 106
LITTLE 18
LITTLE (bit) 18
LIVE 61
LOLLIPOP 39
LONDON 51
LONELY 90
LONG (length) 11
LONG TIME 90
LONG TIME AGO 90
LOOK 90
LOOK AFTER 90
LOSE 14
LOST 62
LORD 64
LORRY 68
LOT (a) 18
LOVE 18
LOVELY 90
LOW 10
LUCKY 63

M

MACHINE 61
MAGAZINE 91
MAGIC 91
MAKE 91
MAN 20
MANAGER 22
MANAGE 54

MANNERS 91
MANY 91
MARK 26
MARKET 51
MARRY .... 21 & 65
MASH 62
MATCH 62
MATERIAL 91
MATHS 24
MATTER (the) 91
MAXIMUM 73
MAYBE 8
MEAL 37
MEAN (imply) 91
MEAN (stingy) 14
MEASURE 24
MEAT 38
MEDAL 63
MEDICINE 57
MEET 91
MEETING 91
MELT 91
MEND 91
MENU 91
MERCY 67
MESS 16
METAL 91
METHOD 91
MEXICO 50
MILE 71
MIDDLE 72
MIGHT 8
MILK 42
MILLION .... 3 & 25
MINE 7
MINIBUS 68
MINICOM 106
MINUTE 28
MINUS 24
MIRROR 73
MISERABLE 92
MISS 91
MISTAKE 91
MITTEN 43
MIX 91
MONEY 54
MONKEY 45
MONTH 29
MOODY 92
MOON 30
MORE 15
MORNING 29
MOST 15
MOTHER 19

MOTORBIKE 68
MOUNTAIN 92
MOUSE 47
MOVE 73
MR. 20
MRS. 20
MUCH 8
MUD 36
MULTIPLY 24
MUSHROOM 41
MUSIC 27
MUST 12
MY 7
MY OWN 7
MYSELF 7

N

NAME 59
NARROW 16
NAUGHTY 92
NAVY 20
NEAR 13
NEARLY 92
NEED 92
NEEDLE 57
NEIGHBOUR 92
NEPHEW 19
NERVOUS 92
NET 63
NEVER 92
NEW 10
NEWS 56
NEWSPAPER 56
NEXT 92
NEXT WEEK 29
NEXT YEAR 29
NICE 18
NIECE 19
NIGHT 28
NIGHT GOWN 44
NINE 2
NINETEEN 2
NINETY 3
NO 92
NO (not any) 92
NOISE 105
NONE 92
NORWAY 50
NOT 92
NOTE (music) 27
NOTHING 16
NOT SURE 13
NOT YET 92

NOW 6
NUMBER .... 69 & 106
NUN 64
NURSE 57
NURSERY 61
NUT 40

O

OATH 66
OBJECT (to) 93
OCCUR 11
O'CLOCK 93
OFF (absent) 53
OFF (cancel) 93
OFF (get off) 17
OFFICE 53
OFTEN 17
OLD 10
ON 17
ONCE 93
ONE 2
ONION 41
ONLY 93
OPEN 15
OPERATION 57
OPPORTUNITY 93
OPPOSE 93
OPPOSITE (idea) 93
OPPOSITE (place) 93
ORAL 93
ORANGE 4
ORANGE JUICE 39
ORDER (arrange) 93
ORDER (command) .. 93
ORGANISE 93
OTHER 93
OTHERS 93
OUR 7
OUT 9
OUTSIDE 11
OVER 17
OVERTAKE 72
OWE 54
OWL 47
OR 93

P

PACK 94
PAGE 23
PAIN 59
PAINT 94
PAIR 94

INDEX

PANIC 94
PAPER 23
PARAGRAPH 23
PARALLEL 94
PARENT 19
PARIS 50
PARK 36
PARK (car) 72
PARROT 48
PART 94
PARTICULAR 94
PARTNER 21
PARTY 39
PASS 72
PAST (the) 94
PASTIES 37
PATIENT (clam) 15
PATTERN 94
PAVEMENT 70
PAY 53
PEAS 41
PEACH 40
PEAR 40
PEDAL-CAR 36
PEN 24
PENCIL 24
PENGUIN 48
PENNY/PENCE 54
PEOPLE 20
PERCENT 24
PERFECT 94
PERHAPS 8
PERSUADE 94
PET 47
PETROL 69
PHOTO 94
PIANO 27
PICNIC 39
PINEAPPLE 40
PINK 4
PIE 38
PIER 51
PIG 46
PILL 58
PILLOW 32
PIPE 94
PIZZA 37
PLACE 94
PLAN 94
PLANT 35
PLASTIC 94
PLATE 33
PLATE (car) 69
PLAY 36

PLEASE 12
PLENTY 95
PLUM 40
PLUS 24
POCKET 44
POEM 95
POINT (make a) 95
POISON 59
POLICE .... 66 & 106
POLICE CAR 68
POLITE 15
POND 36
POOR 15
POORLY 58
POPULAR 95
POSH 95
POSSIBLE 15
POST 56
POST OFFICE 56
POTATO 41
POUND 54
POWER 95
PRACTICE 73
PRAISE 65
PRAM 36
PRAY 64
PREFER 95
PREGNANT 58
PREPARE 95
PRESENT 95
PRETEND 95
PRETTY 18
PRICE 55
PRIEST 64
PRINCE 22
PRINCESS 22
PRINT 56
PRISON 66
PRIVATE 95
PRIZE (trophy) 62
PROBLEM 95
PROFESSIONAL 95
PROFIT 95
PROGRAMME 27
PROMISE 95
PROOF 67
PROTESTANT 64
PUBLICITY 95
PUBLISHED 56
PUDDING 95
PUPPET 95
PURPLE 4
PUT 95
PYJAMAS 44

Q

QUALIFICATIONS 26
QUARREL 96
QUARTER 25
QUEEN 22
QUESTION 26
QUEUE 96
QUICK 10
QUIET 105
QUITE 96

R

RABBIT 47
RADIO 27
RAFFLE 96
RAILWAY 52
RAIN 30
RAINBOW 96
RAINCOAT 43
RAISE 96
RARELY 17
RATHER 96
RAW 96
READ 23
READY 96
REAL/REALLY 96
REASON 96
RECEIVE 13
RECENTLY 96
RECIPE 39
RECOGNISE 96
RED 4
REFLECTION 96
REFUSE 96
REGISTER 96
REGULAR 97
RELATE 97
RELEASE 97
REMEMBER 14
RENT 57
REPEAT 97
REPLY 97
REPRESENT 67
RESIGN 53
RESEARCH 97
RESPONSIBLE 97
REST 57
REVENGE 97
REVERSE 97
RHINOCEROS 45
RICE 42
RICH 15

RIDE 63
RIGHT 5
RING 97
RIPE 40
RISK 97
ROAD (car) 72
ROAST 38
ROCK 51
ROLL 97
ROOF 31
ROOM 31
ROOT 35
ROPE 97
ROUGH 14
ROUND 25
RUBBER 24
RUBBISH (waste) 97
RUDE (manners) 15
RUDE (indecent) 97
RUGBY 62
RULES 97
RULER 24
RUN 14
RUSH 97
RUSSIA 50

S

SACK (to) 53
SAD 12
SAFE 98
SAIL 63
SAILOR 20
SALAD 41
SALT 38
SAME 11
SAND 51
SANDAL 43
SANDWICH 37
SATISFIED 98
SAUCE 38
SAUCER 33
SAUSAGE 37
SAVE 54
SCARE 98
SCARF 43
SCHOOL .... 23 & 52
SCIENCE 25
SCOOTER (toy) 36
SCORE 62
SCOTLAND 50
SCREW 98
SEA 51
SEAL 47

112

INDEX

SEARCH 98
SEASON 30
SEAFOOD 42
SECOND (clock) 28
SECOND (2nd) 98
SECRET 98
SECRETARY 21
SEED 35
SEEM 70
SELF 7
SELFISH 98
SEND 56
SENTENCE 23
SEPARATE 11
SERIES 98
SERIOUS 71
SERVANT 22
SEVEN 2
SEVENTEEN 2
SEVENTY 3
SEW 60
SIX 2
SIXTEEN 2
SIXTY 3
SHADE 98
SHALLOW 11
SHAME (guilt) 67
SHAME (pity) 98
SHARE 98
SHAPE 98
SHAVE 98
SHE 21
SHEEP 46
SHEET 32
SHEPHERD 65
SHIFT (work) 53
SHINE 98
SHIRT 44
SHOCK 98
SHOE 43
SHOP 55
SHOPPING 55
SHORT 11
SHORTS 99
SHOUT 105
SHOW 99
SHOWER 60
SHUT 15
SHY 99
SICK 58
SIDE 72
SIDEBOARD 32
SIGN 26
SIGN (warning) 69

SILENT 105
SILLY 99
SILVER 4
SIMILAR 99
SINCE 99
SING .... 27 & 64
SINGLE (status) 21
SINGLE (one) 70
SINK (kitchen) 33
SISTER 19
SIT 11
SITUATION 70
SKATE 63
SKILL 70
SKIP 63
SKIPPING ROPE 36
SKIRT 43
SKY 70
SLEEP 59
SLIDE 36
SLIP 73
SLIPPER 44
SLOW .... 10 & 72
SMACK 99
SMALL 18
SMART 99
SMOOTH 14
SNAIL 48
SNAKE 47
SNOOKER 62
SNOW 30
SOAP 60
SOCIAL WORKER 65
SOCK 44
SOFA 32
SOFT 99
SOIL 36
SOLDIER 64
SOME 15
SOMEONE 14
SOMETHING 16
SOMETIME 99
SON 19
SONG 64
SOON 99
SORRY 99
SORT OUT 99
SOUL 99
SOUND 105
SOUP 37
SPACE 99
SPADE 35
SPAGHETTI 38

SPAIN 50
SPEAK .... 105 & 106
SPECIAL 61
SPEND 55
SPIDER 48
SPILL 99
SPIT 100
SPLIT 100
SPOIL 100
SPOON 34
SPORT 62
SPROUTS 41
SPOTS 58
SPRING 30
SQUASH 100
SQUARE 25
SQUIRREL 46
STAMP (post) 56
STAND 11
STAIR 31
STAR 29
STARK 100
START .... 17 & 72
STATION 52
STAY 13
STEAL 66
STEEL 100
STICKS 100
STILL 100
STOCKING 43
STOMACH 100
STONE 36
STOP (-go) 72
STOP 100
STORY 23
STRAIGHT 71
STRAWBERRY 40
STRIKE 100
STRING 100
STRONG 10
STUCK 100
STUPID 100
SUBTRACT 24
SUGAR 42
SUIT 43
SUMMER 30
SUN 29
SUNDAY 65
SUNRISE 100
SUPPORT 100
SURE 13
SUSPICIOUS 67
SWAN 48
SWEDEN 50

SWEDE (turnip) 41
SWIM 63
SWITCH 100
SWITZERLAND 50

T

TABLE 32
TABLET 57
TAIL 101
TAKE 13
TAKE IN (absorb) 101
TALE 101
TALL 101
TALK 105
TAXI 68
TEMPT 101
TEA 42
TEACH 23
TEACHER 23
TEAPOT 33
TEAR (rip) 101
TEASE 101
TEA-SET 33
TEASPOON 34
TELEPHONE 106
TELEVISION 27
TELL 101
TEMPORARY 101
TEN 2
TENT 101
TEST 59
THAN 6
THANK YOU 12
THAT 6
THAT'S ALL 6
THEATRE 52
THEIR 6
THEN 6
THEM 6
THEORY 101
THERE 6
THEREFORE 6
THERMOMETER 58
THESE 6
THEY 6
THICK 16
THIEVE 67
THIN 16
THING 8
THINK 26
THIRTEEN 2
THIRTY 3
THIS 6

113

INDEX

THIS WEEK 29
THOROUGH 101
THOSE 6
THOUGHTFUL 101
THOUSAND .... 3 & 25
THREAD 101
THREE 2
THREE-QUARTER 25
THROAT 101
THROUGH 71
THROW 101
THUNDER 30
TICKET 52
TIDY 16
TIE (neck) 44
TIE (string) 102
TIGER 45
TIME 28
TIPPER-LORRY 68
TIRED 59
TITLE 102
TO 13
TOAST 37
TOUCH 102
TODAY 28
TOE 102
TOGETHER 11
TOIL 102
TOILET 60
TOMATO 41
TOMORROW 28
TOP 10
TORMENT 102
TORTOISE 47
TOSS AND TURN 61
TOTAL 54
TOUR 50
TOWARDS 102
TOWEL 60
TOWN 51
TRACTOR 68
TRAFFIC 69
TRAFFIC-LIGHTS 70
TRAIN 69
TRIANGLE 25
TRANSPORT 69
TRAVEL 71
TRAY 33
TREBLE 102
TREE 35
TRIP 102
TROUBLE 67
TROUSER 44
TRUMPET 27

TRUST 102
TRUE 67
TRUTH 67
T-SHIRT 44
TRY 6
TURKEY 46
TURN 71
TWELVE 2
TWENTY 3
TWO 2
TWICE 102

U

UGLY 18
UNCLE 19
UNDER 17
UNDERGROUND TRAIN 102
UNDERNEATH 102
UNDERSTAND .... 60 & 73
UNEMPLOYED 53
UNIFORM 44
UNLESS 68
UNIVERSITY 26
UNTIL 102
UP 17
UPSET 102
US 7
USE 102

V

VALLEY 51
VALUE 55
VARIOUS 103
VEGETABLE 41
VERY 8
VEST 44
VIDEO 27
VILLAGE 51
VINEGAR 42
VISIT 59
VOCABULARY 103
VOICE .... 105 & 106
VOLUNTEER 22
VOTE 103

W

WAGE 53
WAIT 73
WAKE UP 61
WALES 50
WALK 14

WALL 31
WANT 5
WAR 103
WARDROBE 32
WAREHOUSE 52
WARM 61
WARN 69
WAS 8
WASH 60
WASHING MACHINE 33
WASTE 103
WATCH (a) 103
WATCH (to) 103
WATER 103
WAVE 103
WE 7
WEAK 103
WEAR 103
WEATHER 30
WEDDING 65
WEED 103
WEEK 29
WEEKEND 29
WEIGHT 59
WELCOME 103
WELDER 22
WELL 61
WEST 71
WET 60
WHALE 48
WHAT 5
WHAT TIME ? 104
WHEELCHAIR 58
WHEN 5
WHERE 5
WHICH 5
WHILE 103
WHISPER 103
WHISTLE 104
WHITE 4
WHO 5
WHOSE 5
WHY 5
WIDE 16
WIFE 20
WILD 104
WILL 5
WIN 62
WIND 30
WINDOW 31
WINE 39
WING 104
WINTER 30
WIPE 104

WIRE 104
WISH 103
WISE 103
WITH 5
WITCH 104
WITHDRAWN 104
WITHOUT 5
WITNESS 104
WOLF 46
WOMAN 20
WONDERFUL 104
WON'T 5
WOOD 104
WOOL 104
WORD 104
WORK 22
WORLD 50
WORM 46
WORN 104
WORRY 104
WORSE 16
WORST 16
WORTH 55
WOULD 104
WRITE 24
WRONG 5

X

X-RAY 57
XYLOPHONE 27

Y

YEAR 29
YELLOW 4
YES 9
YESTERDAY 28
YOGHURT 42
YOU 7
YOUNG 10
YOUR 7
YOUR OWN 7
YOURSELF 7
YOURSELVES 7

Z

ZEBRA 48
ZERO 2
ZOO 45

114

NOTES